The Crazy World series (Hardback £3.99) There are now 16 different titles in this best-selling cartoon series – one of them must be right for a friend of yours ...

Published in Great Britain in 1988 by Exley Publications Ltd, 16 Chalk Hill, Watford, Herts WD1 4BN, United Kingdom.

ISBN 1-85015-112-1

Printed and bound in Hungary.

the CRAZY world of the OFFICE

**Cartoons by
Bill Stott**

⬛EXLEY

"And this is a more analytical analysis of the analysis you analyzed last week."

"Word processor, printer, fax, electric typewriter, desk top
publishing system, but thumbtacks? No, sorry."

"You must be new here – when I say 'tea or coffee', you don't choose, you guess!"

"*You're right, the fault you reported is basic. It's called 'not-plugged-in'.*"

"You're through to your wife now, Sir..."

*"Get up Creeply, you're not in the office now – just make
sure I win – O.K?"*

"*I'm not sure … ring someone I fired recently – they'll be honest…*"

"Balancing twenty-seven thumbtacks is remarkable, but you must ask yourself if it's exactly beneficial, office-wise, that is..."

"WOW! My in-tray just suffered spontaneous combustion!"

"You have a home computer then?"

"Don't be so dramatic – we all get computer bugs..."

4

5

"Any more objections?"

*"No sir, I did not trip you on purpose. It was an accident
– unfortunately."*

"Wentworth – be a darling and get your mean old lady boss
a cup of tea would you?"

"If letter size equals clout here I don't want to meet the boss..."

"That's the fourth temp it's eaten this week..."

*"Of course I love you more than I love the office.
15.3% in fact."*

"I will not tolerate persistent lateness, Parfitt."

"If the worst comes to the worst, can I have Mr. Travis's parking lot?"

"She's a genius, she's got <u>Dallas</u> on her screen again!"

"It's a little tedium reliever – alternate Tuesdays I can't step on a white tile…"

"Henshaw – if you're inclined toward laying the foundations
of an illicit relationship – I'm free between
3:42p.m. and 4:07p.m."

"The computer's down, my typewriter is missing 'e', it's 5:30 and Ms. Bossy Boots just gave me 28 letters and you bother me with the house burning down?!?"

"Somebody moved my phone again!"

"So then you said – why's a smart chick like you doing a
boring job like this?"

"*I wonder, Miss Flank, if you'd mind accusing me of sexual harassment within earshot of the other blokes?*"

"I had my personal organizer rigged to catch the office mole..."

"Make a note on his file "Hates tea, but scared of the Tea lady."

COMPLAINTS

MINOR NIGGLES

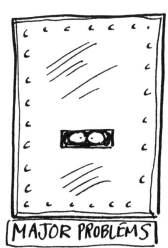

MAJOR PROBLEMS

"I see the guy from accounts upstairs is still crazy about
you…"

"I see Farnsworth finally got the key to the executive washroom.."

"You always were a rebel Spanswick. Just look at your lamp."

"Sensors indicate that No. 2 cubicle has been occupied for eighteen minutes. Do you require assistance?"

"You're the new elevator attendant, right? Guess who's the
boss and who's the secretary. Get it wrong and I'll fire you."

"The chap you're taking over from – we think the plant ate him!"

"Raspberry yogurt and chicken sandwiches – when will he accept that she hates them?"

"*Sometimes, when I get that date stamp in my hand, I come over all peculiar...*"

"It's a pretty good company performance indicator when your head of forward planning pulls this sort of stunt..."

"On a good day you can see clear through the Skrellington
building to the brick wall behind…"

"Mrs. Wainwright? Yes, she's standing by the elevator with that accident prone guy from accounts."

"Take a note – Ponsford is still making P.C. advances toward
Edgely..."

"It's an internal carrier pigeon – we're very green here..."

"I've decided to make a few changes, Miss Spiggot..."

"Look at that – company mortgage, company car, company smirk..."

"And I will not tolerate you spreading stories that I bully women!"

"You dare commit suicide in the company's time and I'll fire you Fittock, d'you hear?"

"Security's attempts to disguise the video cameras as smoke detectors have failed."

"As a temp. there are a few things you should know, like this place is so dull, the plant was just made 'Man of the Year'."

"O.K. who turned the extractor on?"

"Just think – at the push of a button I can send 3000 kilos
of Andulsian lemons speeding to the market places of
north-west Belgium!"

"R.J.'s never been good with people..."

"He likes to make sure the in-tray is really full…"

"Don't clam up on me – I've annoyed you somehow – right?"

"You've read my analysis, then?"

"Acting up again? Allow me..."

1

2

1

"O.K. I need the bottom line on net profit next year."

"What's that weird 'beep beep'?"

3

"That's the closest a MKII A/K 9334/4 gets to sardonic laughter..."

"Boy – when they screw a pen down here, they don't mess around!"

"Freeborn, Snappit and Pont, next door, are complaining about your cheese plant, Ms. Bevis."

1

2

3

"Two things about female bosses, Worthington... One – we are just as fair as men. Two – we are much better liars..."

"You have a problem with becoming our man in the Antarctic, Henshaw?"

"She can take charge of my floppy disk any time."

"At least, I'm not like some guys – when I come home I
leave the office behind – period – sorry, make that a colon
or maybe a comma, or..."

"And what's so interesting about the Skrellington building this morning?"

"The M.D. never could write a concise memo..."

"That'll be a message from the chairperson. She's ultra low tech."

"I can't disturb him – he's thinking up witty things for the ansaphone tape."

"And here's a list of things I don't mind chatting about..."

"Bernard – let's understand something right from the start ... I like to fire people – it makes me feel good – O.K?"

"You're quite right sir, my wife hates my job. Unfortunately,
so do I."

"*I'm sorry, Mr. Finniston can't see anyone right now...*"

"The elevator jammed – and you know K.J. – he never could delegate..."

"They don't tolerate bad time keeping here, do they?"

"Flow-chart, flow-chart on the wall who is the boredest of them all?"

"With reference to what you said at the office party. This is my mother."

"And with a defiant shout, the chief clerk hurled the floppy disk across the typing pool. It struck the manager a sickening blow, she fell into the shredder and was never seen again!"

"And all that rubbish about placing the interviewee on a lower chair to make him feel inferior ... quite the opposite is true..."

"I know it's 5:29p.m., Tootsie. I know it's Friday. I know you worked late last night. However..."

"I'm going home. I just ran my lunch through the shredder."

"6:00p.m. I start. If you're still here, you get your feet vacuumed."

Other books in the "Crazy World" series:

The Crazy World of Birdwatching. £3.99. By Peter Rigby. Over eighty cartoons on the strange antics of the twitcher brigade. One of our most popular pastimes, this will be a natural gift for any birdwatcher.

The Crazy World of Gardening. £3.99. By Bill Stott. The perfect present for anyone who has ever wrestled with a lawnmower that won't start, over-watered a pot plant or been assaulted by a rose bush from behind.

The Crazy World of Golf. £3.99. By Mike Scott. Over eighty hilarious cartoons show the fanatic golfer in his (or her) every absurdity. What really goes on out on the course, and the golfer's life when not playing are chronicled in loving detail.

The Crazy World of The Handyman. £3.99. By Roland Fiddy. This book is a must for anyone who has ever hung *one* length of wallpaper upside down or drilled through an electric cable. A gift for anyone who has ever tried to "do it yourself" and failed!

The Crazy World of Jogging. £3.99. By David Pye. An ideal present for all those who find themselves running early in the morning in the rain and wondering why they're there. They'll find their reasons, their foibles and a lot of laughs in this book.

The Crazy World of Love. £3.99. By Roland Fiddy. This funny yet tender collection covers every aspect of love from its first joys to its dying embers. An ideal gift for lovers of all ages to share with each other.

The Crazy World of Marriage. £3.99. By Bill Stott. The battle of the sexes in close-up from the altar to the grave, in public and in private, in and out of bed. See your friends, your enemies (and possibly yourselves?) as never before!

The Crazy World of Music. £3.99. By Bill Stott. This upbeat collection will delight music-lovers of all ages. From Beethoven to Wagner and from star conductor to the humblest orchestra member, no-one escapes Bill Stott's penetrating pen.

The Crazy World of Photography. £3.99. By Bill Stott. Everyone who owns a camera, be it a Box Brownie or the latest Pentax, will find something to laugh at in this superb collection. The absurdities of the camera freak will delight your whole family.

The Crazy World of Rugby. £3.99. By Bill Stott. From schoolboy to top international player, no-one who plays or watches rugby will escape Bill Stott's merciless exposé of their habits and absurdities. Over 80 hilarious cartoons – a must for all addicts.

The Crazy World of Sailing. £3.99. By Peter Rigby. The perfect present for anyone who has ever messed about in boats, gone pea-green in a storm or been stuck in the doldrums.

The Crazy World of Sex. £3.99. By David Pye. A light-hearted look at the absurdities and weaker moments of human passion – the turn-ons and the turn-offs. Very funny and in (reasonably) good taste.

The Crazy World of Skiing. £3.99. By Craig Peterson and Jerry Emerson. Covering almost every possible (and impossible) experience on the slopes, this is an ideal present for anyone who has ever strapped on skis – and instantly fallen over.

The Crazy World of Tennis. £3.99. By Peter Rigby. Would-be Pat Cashes and Chris Everts watch out.... This brilliant collection will pin-point their pretensions and poses. Whether you play yourself or only watch on TV, this will amuse and entertain you!

United Kingdom
These books make super presents. Order them from your local bookseller or from Exley Publications Ltd, Dept BP, 16 Chalk Hill, Watford, Herts WD1 4BN. (Please send £1.00 to cover post and packing.)
United States
All these titles are distributed in the United States by Slawson Communications Inc., 165 Vallecitos de Oro, San Marcos, CA92069 and are priced at $8.95 each.